# A Lifetime of Practice

Awakened Heart Sangha

'To create a presence in the world of a genuine connection to Awakening for those who are seeking it'

Published by

The Shrimala Trust

Criccieth, Gwynedd UK

www.ahs.org.uk

Email: office@ahs.org.uk

First published April 2015


The Shrimala Trust is a registered charity (No. 1078783)
and a limited company (No. 3880647)
which supports the activity of the Awakened Heart Sangha.
The Awakened Heart Sangha is a spiritual community
under the direction of Lama Shenpen Hookham.

# Contents

# Preface

This book aims to act as a guide to the practice and structure of the Awakened Heart Sangha for its current and prospective students and Members. With a clear overview like this, you will be in a position to decide at what point you might want to move towards a deeper commitment and involvement in the teachings, community and activities of the Awakened Heart Sangha.

Producing and distributing this book is the first step in clarifying a dynamic structure that has been emerging organically over the past 15 years or more in my vision for a Sangha here in the West – a Sangha of scattered Members with largely different lifestyles, time commitments and levels of understanding of the Dharma.

The Awakened Heart Sangha is a community of non-monastic Kagyu-Nyingma of the Tibetan tradition, informed by all the blessing, principles and teachings of the lineage and yet having to forge our own path into the high-tech, uncertain and rapidly changing world of the 21st Century.

We, in the West, have a rich culture of our own and yet lack the essential teachings for inner peace and liberation. That is why, over the last 50 years I have devoted myself to the study and practice of these teachings. Since being asked by my teachers to teach in the West, I have grappled with what it is that Westerners really need to know and how to provide it.

As H.E. Khandro Rinpoche says, the teachings have been taking hold in the West for a century. The challenge now is to create a Sangha, more specifically for us a Mahayana Sangha that meets our needs.

This book is a step towards a master plan for such a Sangha and the details will have to be worked out gradually and refined over time.

Lama Shenpen Hookham – 2015.

## The Awakened Heart Sangha is a Mandala

The Awakened Heart Sangha is a mandala of students, teachers and supporters dedicated to the Path of Awakening. The mandala is continually evolving around the core principle of Openness, Clarity and Sensitivity.

The Path of Awakening operates by means of transmission as we discover in our experience the Truth, which goes beyond birth and death.

Each person in the mandala helps create and maintain the mandala as a vehicle to carry the transmission, for their own sake and for the sake of all beings.

# Outline of the Structure of the Awakened Heart Sangha

As this diagram shows, the Awakened Heart Sangha has 5 main circles that make up the structure of the mandala. The lineage is the centre of the mandala, which permeates the entire structure.

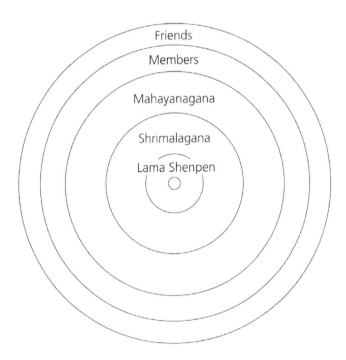

**Friends** - The Awakened Heart Sangha welcomes anyone as a Friend who supports and participates in any part of its activity, including volunteering to help in various ways and contributing financially.

**Members** – Those who have formally requested to become students of Lama Shenpen and have committed to practise within the Sangha.

**The Mahayanagana** – Those Members who have formally committed themselves to connecting with each other and deepening their practice, creating a vehicle for the transmission lineage.

**The Shrimalagana** – The heart of the Mahayanagana. Its Members are recognised as having the integrity to stand for the values and ethos of the mandala. They have made a formal commitment to carrying the responsibility for the long-term future of Lama Shenpen's vision for the Sangha.

**Lama Shenpen** is at the centre of the mandala, representing the lineage of teachers and teachings that connect us to Awakening.

She creates and maintains the Mandala of the Awakened Heart Sangha as a vehicle to transmit the power of Dharma to this and future generations.

She operates by means of the spiritual transmission she has received from the lineage of her teachers.

## Lineage Connections

Lama Shenpen's teachings come from her own training in the Kagyu-Nyingma lineages of Tibetan Buddhism.

Following meditation instruction from Trungpa Rinpoche, Karma Thinley Rinpoche, Bokar Rinpoche and Kalu Rinpoche, she took ordination as a nun from HH 16th Karmapa in India, who subsequently asked her to return to the West to teach.

Having spent several years as a translator for Gendun Rinpoche, she met her current teacher Khenpo Tsultrim Gyamtso Rinpoche who authorised her to teach Mahamudra. She also met and married Rigdzin Shikpo, a senior student of Trungpa Rinpoche. Rigdzin Shikpo subsequently became one of her main teachers.

Following advice from the teacher of all her teachers, HH Dilgo Khyentse Rinpoche she established a retreat centre and built a stupa in North West Wales.

She developed Discovering the Heart of Buddhism as a way of bringing the foundational principles of the Dharma to Western students and continues to train her students in meditation, reflection and insight using the framework of the Tibetan Mahamudra tradition.

For more information on Lama Shenpen and her teachers – **www.ahs.org.uk.**

## The Hermitage

The Hermitage is Lama Shenpen's residence where she spends most of her time in retreat and working with her students and on her writing.

As the sacred space at the centre of the mandala, the Hermitage fulfils a vital role in supporting Lama Shenpen and the senior students who live and practise with her. It is the hub of practice within the Sangha, with meditation, study and reflection continuing daily and can accommodate up to 25 people on group retreats, or several solitary retreatants at any one time.

The Hermitage is regarded as a sacred space, because of the Dharma practice that takes place and especially because it has a fully consecrated Stupa containing the relics of many great Buddhist teachers. The relics go back to the Buddha Shakyamuni himself, and include many of the Karmapas as well as HH Khyentse Rinpoche, Trungpa Rinpoche, Bokar Rinpoche and many others. At its heart is a smaller stupa consecrated by Khenpo Tsultrim Gyamtso Rinpoche.

Lama Shenpen encourages all of her students to spend time practising at the Hermitage.

The Hermitage is open to visitors by appointment. It acts as a resource for the local community and is a regular venue for meditation days that are open to anyone, regardless of experience. *You can find out more about the Hermitage and the Stupa online – www.ahs.org.uk*

# The Path to Awakening

## Freeing Oneself and Others from Samsara

The Awakened Heart Sangha exists to make the genuine transmission of the Truth of the Dharma available for those who are seeking it.

The Dharma has one purpose: to realize the Truth of Awakening. It means Awakening to the Truth that goes beyond birth and death - the Unborn, Nirvana.

'Dharma' means both the Truth of Awakening - and the Path to realizing it within oneself.

It requires us to radically change our way of being and thinking. For this we need conviction and commitment. It is not just about this life but our future lives too and eventually liberation from samsara for ourselves and all beings.

Since death comes without warning, we need to be ready on a daily basis, at whatever level of practice, to face death with confidence. Practising Dharma is therefore about facing our own mortality.

All aspects of practice are ways to strengthen our confidence in the Dharma should we die this very day. We can never simply sit back and think 'Death won't come today'. We need to be ready for it - always.

Following the path to Awakening is not like training to pass exams or gather credentials. It is more challenging than that.

Everyone progresses in their own way. While we endeavour to understand the teachers and to follow their instructions, ultimately, we can only deepen our understanding and practice ourselves.

# How Are the Teachings Delivered?

**Buddhism Connect** – Weekly email teachings from Lama Shenpen, where she answers questions from her students. These are often framed around *Discovering the Heart of Buddhism* principles, and can reflect on our lives and how to apply the principles in our daily lives.

**Hermitage Retreats and Events** – Throughout the year, Members of the Sangha can co-operate with the residents to organize retreats at the Hermitage. Members and visitors are welcome to attend daily meditation sessions and various other events on the programme through the course of the year.

**Regional Retreats and Events** – Lama Shenpen and other teachers will teach at local groups when requested and suitable arrangements are made. Such events, whether an evening talk, a day of meditation or a residential weekend, provide much needed opportunities for Sangha Members and Friends to come together to practise, hear and discuss the Dharma and strengthen Dharma connections.

*More guidelines and materials on how Members can do this are available. Ask a member of the Shrimalagana or Student Support if you would like more information on organising an event in your area.*

**Live Streaming** – Lama Shenpen gives public talks that are broadcast on the Hermitage website, often on a monthly basis. Some teachings related to the online courses are also broadcast and those who are taking part in the course are invited to watch live. Some study courses are also broadcast live so that Members who can't make it to the Hermitage can take part.

**Online Courses** – The forums on the Sangha website hold study materials that are made into study and discussion courses for groups and individuals to work with. These often include extracts from audio recordings and written teachings that are specifically selected to highlight certain *'Living the Awakened Heart'* areas. These are available for Members only.

**Video and Audio** – A growing number of teachings have been filmed and put on YouTube. Some of these are made available for the public. Most recordings are restricted for Members to access in the archives, which hold hundreds of audio and video recordings from Lama Shenpen's talks and teaching retreats.

**Books and Materials** – there is a wealth of teachings in print and online. Lama Shenpen has written a number of books to help her students engage with the various areas of training. You can access all of these books online or through Student Support.

**Local Groups** – students who live in relative proximity to each other and wish to develop their connections can form a group where they can practise together and discuss the teachings. Members are also encouraged to invite teachers to work through materials or help with setting up meditation and *Discovering the Heart of Buddhism* courses.

*Ask a member of the Shrimalagana or Student Support if you would like more information on setting up a local group.*
*You can find out more details on the website – www.ahs.org.uk*
*Lama Shenpen makes herself available for interviews with Members, prospective students, Hermitage visitors and retreatants whenever she can.*

*For more information on the Shrimalagana – see page 49*

# The Key Features of Training and Practice Within the Awakened Heart Sangha

- **Transmission and Gateways**
- **Spiral Learning**
- **Awakening Dialogue**

## Transmission

You may have read various Awakened Heart Sangha books available online or in print, such as Introduction to Formless Meditation and Discovering the Heart of Buddhism. To engage fully, these teachings require more than simply reading a book. It requires the process of transmission, the power of the living truth passing from person to person. This is called 'lineage transmission' and can take place in various ways and on various levels.

The Awakened Heart Sangha is centred on Lama Shenpen - the representative of the lineage as the source of the living transmission.

She gives the Sangha its vision and authenticity. She has been authorised by all her teachers and by Khenpo Tsultrim Gyamtso Rinpoche in particular, to give transmission of Mahamudra.

She is also authorised to permit others to give transmission.

Because of this, given the right circumstances, the Awakened Heart Sangha is able to pass on a certain level of transmission through Lama Shenpen's lineage connection.

Transmission happens by degrees. It requires a lineage of genuine practitioners with the spiritual power to transmit Awakening. Even though each practitioner, individually may not have the full realisation, the power of the full realisation can pass from one individual to the next through their 'samaya' connection with the lineage. 'Samaya' is a heart connection that is real. It is not a conceptual contrivance.

Ultimately transmission sparks genuine realisation of the Truth of Awakening within oneself.

At the moment that a genuine practitioner gives a transmission you are directly connected to the reality of the power of the lineage. Transmission can take the form of a ritual or a pointing out instruction given either formally or informally. Transmissions are like gateways into the essence of the teachings.

As a member of the Awakened Heart Sangha you will have the opportunity to deepen your connection to this transmission process by preparing yourself to pass through various gateways. These reflect your deepening understanding and commitment to the path of Awakening. The transmission is the beginning of a continuing process of deepening your meditation and daily life practice.

# Gateways

The term 'gateway' in the context of the Awakened Heart Sangha refers to points of transition from one level of engagement within the community to another.

For example, the transition to becoming a Member: you may have connected with the Awakened Heart Sangha by sampling its teachings online, in print, attending events or at a local group. While you may be receiving great benefit from this, at this stage you are still on the edge of the mandala of the AHS, possibly a Friend – however you are not a Member. To become a Member you pass through a gateway and formally become one of Lama Shenpen's students. As a Member you are becoming more engaged and are integral to the energy flow of the shared mandala.

*Read more about Membership on pages 19 and 63*

Having been a Member for a while, you may consider passing through other gateways. You will be required to pause and think about the level of your commitment and whether you understand what it is you are taking on. In the Awakened Heart Sangha these gateways are associated with deepening understanding and a sense of responsibility and transmission. They represent a deepening of the samaya within the student-teacher relationship and with the lineage, the source of transmission.

*Read more about Gateways on page 51*

## Spiral Learning

For most of us, learning has been presented to us as 'linear'. At school we began in the infants and worked our way up; we had to complete one level or topic before moving on to the next, perhaps having to pass an exam on it.

However, learning tends to be 'spiral' rather than linear. As we return to the same teachings over and over again our understanding deepens. Deepening our understanding of any one of a series of topics or principles simultaneously deepens our understanding of them all.

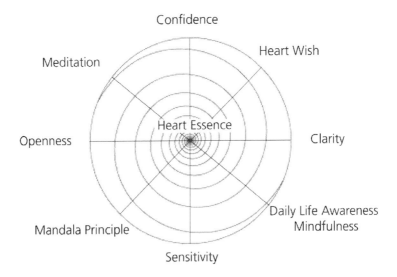

The different themes all lead to a deepening understanding of the Heart Essence, the reality from which they all emanate or emerge.

This is the approach to learning in the Awakened Heart Sangha. It is not a process of hoops and hurdles, acquiring knowledge and credentials. In Dharma it is a deepening process of discovering and trusting the Buddha Nature within ourselves.

Because of the principle of Spiral Learning, most teachings and events in the Awakened Heart Sangha are open to everyone.

## Awakening Dialogue

The Mandala of the Awakened Heart Sangha is created and strengthened by the depth of connections between its Members. Therefore the way we relate to one another is of great importance, whether in peer-peer or teacher-student relationships.

The spirit of open dialogue and inquiry runs through the entire Buddhist tradition: the Buddha didn't preach, but rather taught through skilful questioning and debating key points of the Dharma.

The art of discovering Truth through dialoguing is also in the very foundations of the Western culture we grew up in. Mastery of free inquiry as means to Truth was reached by Socrates and Plato, and is respected in teacher-student relationships, where deep insights often arise as a result of a nurtured Dharma relationship and the art of compassionate communication. It can be a path to Awakening in itself.

To honour this tradition we encourage all students to engage in training courses on Awakening Dialogue and Mentoring.

*You can read more about Mentors on page 40*

# What Membership of the Awakened Heart Sangha Means

As a Member you make a formal commitment to becoming a student of Lama Shenpen and to practising the Dharma as taught within the Awakened Heart Sangha, for the foreseeable future.

You also begin to learn about the values of the Sangha and commit to supporting its activity through your personal practice, service and financial contribution.

To become a Member, you will be expected to receive the transmission of Formless Meditation instructions and to commit to working through the *Discovering the Heart of Buddhism* material with a Mentor.

*Read more about Mentors on page 40*

To begin with your Membership commitment can be relatively light. You can take up to a year to decide if you would like to commit to being recognised as a Member. This will give you time to get to know others in the Sangha and become familiar with its structure and the *Living the Awakened Heart* teachings. Once you decide you would like to be recognised by others as a Member, you will be expected to receive the transmission of *Discovering the Heart of Buddhism* from Lama Shenpen at the annual *Discovering the Heart of Buddhism* retreat at the Hermitage. If your circumstances make this impossible, provisions can be made to make the transmission accessible online or over the phone.

Once you become a Member, you will be able to access the archive of hundreds of recordings, audio and video, as well as participate in online study and practice courses.

As a Member you can arrange one-on-one meditation interviews with Lama Shenpen.

Any mandala consists of a central principle around which the main body of the mandala builds itself. The main body of the AHS mandala is its Members. It can only function by the commitment, practice and contribution of its Members. The Members are expected to see service to the Sangha as part of their practice. This means that Members take on various roles that support the activity of the Awakened Heart Sangha as their circumstances allow. These roles are as varied as the skills and capacity of the Members themselves, from running or helping at an event or local group, transcribing or digitizing talks to simply being a supportive presence.

Members make a regular financial contribution. They recognise that the Sangha's activity is wholly reliant on the generosity of its Members and Friends.

*There is more detailed information on how to become a Supporting Friend or Member or how make a donation from page 63.*

## Personal Pathway

When you become a Member, the question arises – "what is my pathway of practice?"

The pathway consists of 3 different areas:

1: Personal Practice

- Meditation and Retreat
- Study and Reflection
- Taking Vows

2: Companionship and Sangha

- Awakening Dialogue
- Service as Practice
- Local Groups
- Retreats and Events
- Online Forums and Discussion Groups

3: Deepening commitment within the Sangha

- Ganas and Structure of the Sangha
- Gateways
- Mentorship

## Personal Practice

The complete practice in the Awakened Heart Sangha is called 'Living the Awakened Heart' – Members receive a booklet with this title. It encapsulates the whole range of teachings within the Buddhist tradition.

As described earlier, spiral learning means that you can approach any of the areas of practice at any time, as teachings are made available. You can go at your own pace.

You will be given a 'Personal Pathway folder'. It is recommended that you keep a record of your practice and learning and write down any questions that may come up for you to discuss with your Mentor or Lama Shenpen. You can also keep a record of any interviews you have had with Lama Shenpen, or a diary of the conversations you have with your Mentor.

The Personal Pathway folder also gives advice on suggested reading and ways in which you can reflect on the whole range of teachings in the Buddhist tradition and how they relate to each other and your current practice.

It is important to keep in mind that, while it may appear to be a 'record of achievement', it is really a way of helping you to navigate areas of practice that are available to you.

For example, your main focus of practice might be *Discovering the Heart of Buddhism*. It is more than likely that you will be attending teaching events that touch on other areas of the training. By keeping a record of these events in your Personal Pathway folder, you can see how your training is developing and deepening, and in which areas. It is meant to be an inspiring way of reflecting on your practice rather than a list of achievements, and the aim is that it will galvanise your practice and help to focus your discussions with your Mentor.

# Retreat as a Way of Strengthening and Deepening Your Practice

Retreat means setting time aside to stay in one place to focus on your formal practice of study, reflection and meditation on Dharma. Being on retreat helps to deepen and strengthen your practice.

In the Buddhist tradition some yogins stay in retreat for years, decades or even their whole lifetime. It is more common to stay in retreat for shorter periods such as a week or a month or several months. It is good to begin with very short retreats such as a day or even half a day. Sometimes this is all the time that our busy lives will allow for and yet this can still be very worthwhile.

Retreats can be held at home or anywhere where you are not going to be disturbed. It is good to try to pencil in regular retreats throughout the course of the year and to give them priority when planning your time. Unless you make a real effort to value them is easy for other things to take over.

We can value retreat as a way of benefitting others as well as ourselves. It is important to reflect on the truth of this.

Group retreats are held on a fairly regular basis at the Hermitage but can be arranged anywhere. It is simply a matter of somebody pulling a team together to organize them. Nevertheless, Lama Shenpen does want all her students to visit the Hermitage and the Stupa to practise there for at least a few days, to get a feel of the place and contribute to its atmosphere. If you make a point of visiting it annually that is even better.

When doing a retreat it is important to set yourself a program and if possible get it approved by Lama Shenpen or a Senior Mentor. This can be an opportunity to provide you with encouragement, advice and also reassurance that your retreat is recognized and so that others can rejoice in your commitment.

It is good to take commitment vows before the retreat and to finish with giving back the vows and dedicating the 'punya' (Tib: Sonam – often translated as merit, benefit or the 'power of goodness')

There is a booklet called 'Mandala of Sacred Space' in print and Kindle that you can read to understand some of these aspects better and for ideas on how you might structure your time.

## Training in 'Living the Awakened Heart'

As mentioned earlier, the overall training in the Awakened Heart Sangha is called 'Living the Awakened Heart'.

This consists of working with the following areas of practice with an approach based on the principles of spiral learning and transmission.

It all begins with *Formless Meditation* and broadens out into the fundamental principles outlined in *Discovering the Heart of Buddhism*.

These are further deepened and expanded in *Trusting the Heart of Buddhism* and the other areas of *Living the Awakened Heart*.

All *Living the Awakened Heart* practices include all of the principles found in *Discovering the Heart of Buddhism*.

Everything you are learning and practising in *Living the Awakened Heart* is for helping you develop ever greater confidence in the Indestructible Heart Essence, the true nature of your being: the Non-Conditioned, the Unborn.

- **Introduction to Formless Meditation**
  - The Essence of Meditation
  - Sitting Meditation
  - Walking Meditation
  - Daily Life Awareness
  - Establishing A Daily Practice
  - Deepening Your Practice
  - Developing Insight
- **Discovering the Heart of Buddhism**
  - Indestructible Heart Essence
  - Heart Wish
  - Confidence
  - Openness
  - Clarity
  - Sensitivity
  - Mandala Principle
- **Trusting the Heart of Buddhism**
  - Truth Is The Nature Of Reality
  - Truth Is Alive Not An Abstraction
  - Truth Is What You Become
  - Truth Is What You Are Possessed By

- There Is A Path That Leads To The Realization Of Truth
- The Path Flows From The Truth
- Truth As Emanation
- Truth Draws Us To Itself
- The Truth Has Protective Power
- Truth Is What We Have Always Been

- **Further Areas of Training**
  - Love And Compassion
  - Insight Into Emptiness
  - Daily Life Awareness and Mindfulness Practice
  - Vaster Vision
  - Making Pranidhanas
  - Making Connections
  - Death And Dying

Each of the areas is a full practice in itself and informs the others.

All materials, events and retreats elaborate on one or more of these areas.

## Introduction to Formless Meditation

The practice of Formless Meditation is the basis for all other teachings within the Awakened Heart Sangha. Taking the principles of Formless Meditation into your daily life is called 'Daily Life Awareness'. This is often called 'Mindfulness' in other contexts.

You would normally have received the transmission for this before becoming a Member as it is the essential first step for all Members of the Sangha.

The transmission will have been given to you in the context of a specific meditation course in which your Mentor introduces you to the practice. This needs to be someone who has a deep confidence in Lama Shenpen, has reached a certain level of training and has been authorized to give an initial transmission until you can receive it from Lama Shenpen in person.

There is a booklet called *Introduction to Formless Meditation* that you might have read. You are recommended to return to it on a regular basis. Even after years of practice it is important to continue to reflect on the exercises in the second part of the book called 'Deepening your Practice' and discuss your experience with your Mentor or Lama Shenpen.

The meditation practice is referred to as Formless Meditation because this is the term Rigdzin Shikpo and his teacher Chögyam Trungpa Rinpoche used. It is used to refer to the core meditation that everyone needs to practise in order to realize Awakening.

Everyone in the Awakened Heart Sangha engages with this meditation. It includes a whole range of practices such as calming the mind, reflection and insight. It ranges from investigation into the views we hold that prevent us from awakening to resting effortlessly in the Awakened Heart. Eventually it could be Mahamudra or Dzogchen – the highest realization of the nature of mind.

## Transmission and meditation interviews with Lama Shenpen

From time to time Lama Shenpen gives transmission for Formless Meditation and also transmissions for the different stages of meditation on Emptiness - or pointing out instructions - within the Mahamudra tradition. These transmissions are sometimes given formally and will be announced as such. Sometimes they are given informally one to one in meditation interviews.

You can read more about preparing for an interview with Lama Shenpen in your Personal Pathway folder.

## Discovering the Heart of Buddhism

The transmission of *Discovering the Heart of Buddhism* marks the formal point of entry into the mandala as a Member. Because it is such an important step, even if you have been through *Discovering the Heart of Buddhism* on your own, to engage in it fully, Members are normally required to work through it with a mentor and to receive the transmission from Lama Shenpen at the first opportunity.

The transmission for *Discovering the Heart of Buddhism* is given at an annual retreat held at the Hermitage.

The principles of *Discovering the Heart of Buddhism* are the core of the Living the Awakened Heart training, so they are all you ever have to work on as a Member of the Awakened Heart Sangha. The themes come up again and again in all areas of practice: in fact, every area of Living the Awakened Heart is intended to deepen your understanding of *Discovering the Heart of Buddhism.*

Because *Discovering the Heart of Buddhism* is built on the principle of spiral learning you start with the essence, the Heart. As you work through the themes of the course, your initial understanding of that essence deepens, until at the end you are ready to start the course again, returning to all the same themes with greater understanding and increasing depth and conviction.

Going back to the beginning is what it is all about. Progress is not about how much you have learnt, but how deeply you understand and can apply the principles with which you began.

It pays to go back over the principles of *Discovering the Heart of Buddhism* again and again, because they point to deep truths that take the whole of one's life to assimilate.

In fact, they point to the very essence of the Buddhist tradition, the Indestructible Heart Essence - which is the essence of Mahamudra and Dzogchen.

## Trusting the Heart of Buddhism

At some point, when you are sufficiently familiar with *Discovering the Heart of Buddhism*, you will need to have a discussion with your mentor about what happens next. Though you may wish to continue working with the same materials for many years, you might feel inspired to engage in *Trusting the Heart of Buddhism*.

Using a similar format to *Discovering the Heart of Buddhism*, it helps you explore within your own experience the vaster and deeper implications of *Discovering the Heart of Buddhism*.

*Trusting the Heart of Buddhism* is an excellent precursor to spiralling back into *Discovering the Heart of Buddhism* and to understanding each of the principles in perhaps an entirely new and more profound way.

Transmission for *Trusting the Heart of Buddhism* is given at retreats at the Hermitage, which may not be held every year, so you might have to wait for an opportunity to receive it.

*Trusting the Heart of Buddhism* paves the way for a profound and extensive understanding of all the teachings within *Living the Awakened Heart* and the Buddhist tradition as a whole.

# Further Areas of Living the Awakened Heart

Formless Meditation, *Discovering the Heart of Buddhism* and *Trusting the Heart of Buddhism* are integral to *Living the Awakened Heart*, the name for a whole lifetime of practice within the Awakened Heart Sangha.

There are seven main areas of training in *Living the Awakened Heart*, corresponding to whole groups of practices and activities found within traditional Buddhist communities. In short they are:

- *Love and Compassion* – The practice common to all great spiritual traditions that underpins the whole Path to Awakening.

- *Insight* Into Emptiness or Nature of Mind – this practice is distinctively Buddhist. It cuts through confusion and is the immediate cause of Awakening and thus liberation from samsara. In Tibetan Buddhism this includes pointing out instructions.

- *Daily Life Awareness Practice* – applying practice within our daily life. This area of practice is about mindfulness of body, speech and mind and how to use whatever situation you are in as Dharma practice. It is about generosity, discipline and patience and so on. It covers a range of areas such as body awareness, truthful and sensitive communication, the precepts, Dharma art and so on. All these practices relate to a deeper understanding of our personal mandala of body, speech, mind/heart and environment. They make immediate sense in terms of leading a happy life and are not necessarily in themselves Buddhist or conducive to the goal of liberation from samsara. In the Awakened Heart Sangha we seek to extend them by linking them to the other areas of *Living the Awakened Heart* so that they are conducive to Liberation.

• *There is More to Dying than Death* - At whatever stage in your practice you are, you are advised to read the book entitled 'There is More to Dying than Death'. This gives you the basic orientation and information you need for facing life and death and incorporating the awareness of the inevitability of death into the whole of your path. You are advised to return to it often and at least on an annual basis. Around the time of celebrating the Buddha's Enlightenment and the consecration of the Stupa at the Hermitage, the Sangha holds a day on which we reflect on death, those who have died and how to prepare for our own death.

In order to make sense of taking Refuge in the Buddha, Dharma and Sangha, we have to understand the depth and scope of the Buddhist worldview. We need to understand how it describes the Path to Awakening and how to engage in it. The following three areas of training deepen our understanding of that worldview and the path, including the meaning of the Three Refuges and how they are able to protect and guide us in this life and beyond.

- *Vaster Vision* of the Buddhist Worldview – studying and reflecting on the teachings in Buddhist sutras and commentaries that describe and explain the stages of the Path of Awakening and Liberation, including karma, and how ignorance and clinging tie us to endless rebirths in samsara.

- *Making Pranidhanas* (vows, resolves, aspirations or wishing prayers) – the practice that focuses, strengthens and drives all our practice day and night and includes honing our motivation and vision, taking vows such as Refuge and Bodhisattva Vows, making prayers and aspirations, reciting liturgy and so on.

- *Making Connections* in Order to Intensify Punya (the power of goodness) and adhishtana (blessing power) – this is about applying Mandala Principle in relation to the Mandala of Awakening. All Buddhist ritual and customs relate to this. It includes relating to teachers and realised beings, sacred objects, substances, sounds and places, life-stories and so on, through making offerings, prostrations or circumambulations etc.

# Vajrayana Practice

The Awakened Heart Sangha belongs to the Kagyu-Nyingma lineages, which are famous for Vajrayana teachings that include Mahamudra and Dzogchen.

Because of its lineage connections, the Awakened Heart Sangha is pervaded by the blessing and influence of the Vajrayana, even though students may not explicitly practice Vajrayana as such.

Nonetheless, Lama Shenpen sometimes introduces specific Vajrayana practices.

*To find out more, please contact Student Support.*

# Refuge and Bodhisattva Vows

Each year, Lama Shenpen gives Refuge and Bodhisattva Vows to those who feel they are ready and inspired to at the Annual Sangha Celebration. This ceremony is held in front of the Stupa at the Hermitage, around the time of Buddha's Enlightenment at the full moon in May or June, which increases the power of the vow.

There are booklets available that give more detail on what taking these vows means and you can find video teachings from Lama Shenpen on YouTube taken from talks she gives each year.

*For more information, see the Book List on page 75.*

# Dharma Companionship Within the Awakened Heart Sangha

Lama Shenpen is particularly concerned about finding ways that Members can have meaningful and in-depth exchanges with each other over the long term to strengthen a sense of Dharma companionship within the Awakened Heart Sangha.

Practically, since everyone is spiralling around the same topics again and again, the whole Sangha community can join in almost any event or retreat and find inspiration and new understandings at their own level of practice. This means that most events, retreats, online courses, materials and so on can be open to all Members. There are many practical advantages to this:

- It is bonding for the whole Sangha

- Newcomers can learn from the more senior Members

- Newer Members who are already quite experienced are not held back as would happen in a linear structure

- A strong sense of spiritual community is fostered

- Everyone is free to develop at their own pace according to their situation without getting left behind if they miss certain events and courses

## Mentorship

Whatever stage a student is at, there is much to be learned by working with others. Each Member commits to working through *Discovering the Heart of Buddhism* with a Senior Mentor. This is someone who has worked through *Discovering the Heart of Buddhism* and has trained to become an Awakened Heart Sangha Mentor.

Partnering with a Mentor helps both of you to deepen your understanding of the principles by focusing on and sharing your experience and understanding of them.

## What Is a Mentor?

A Mentor in the Awakened Heart Sangha is someone who acts as a guide and friend on your path.

Your Mentor is someone who walks with you, with whom you can share experiences and explore questions. This can be a formal or informal arrangement. Informally, this can simply be a sharing of experience with another Sangha Member.

Some Members will have been trained and formally recognised as Mentors. Whether they are a Peer Mentor or a Senior Mentor, their job is not to give you all the answers, but to help you find those answers within yourself.

# Peer Mentors

As you've seen, the Awakened Heart Sangha is divided into circles. A Peer Mentor is someone within the Sangha who is probably within the same circle as you.

They may have a little more experience within the Sangha, but peer-mentoring is generally a collaboration, with two people exploring their learning together.

Many of our online courses take a peer-mentoring approach, with participants pairing up to share experiences, questions and learning.

# Senior Mentors

A Senior Mentor is likely to be someone in a more central circle of the mandala. They may have a wider and deeper understanding of the Awakened Heart Sangha and Lama Shenpen's teachings, though not always a wider or deeper understanding of Dharma practice in general.

A Senior Mentor will guide you in much the same way as a Peer Mentor, but will be able to use their own experience to help you to ask the right questions and explore the most helpful areas.

Any Member wishing to enter one of the Ganas normally has a Senior Mentor from that Gana to help and support them.

There are different Mentors for different roles within the Mandala, some requiring more specific skills than others. All of our Mentors train in the foundation of Awakening Dialogue and many do further training to develop skills required for their particular role.

## Service as Practice

*Living the Awakened Heart* is also about belonging to a spiritual community.

This relates to the area of Daily Life Awareness Practice within *Living the Awakened Heart* training.

Serving the Sangha through volunteering, donation and stepping forward to take responsibility for its future are ways of:

- Strengthening our personal connection to the Sangha
- Ensuring that it continues to exist in the world
- Upholding its values
- Helping others as well as ourselves

Working together with others in this way is a practice in itself which can be joyful as well as throw into sharp relief all our conflicts and assumptions.

There is always work to be done: helping to co-ordinate and run a local group or events, helping to transcribe recordings of teachings, helping to maintain the Hermitage – and, in time, perhaps training as a Mentor or local group leader.

At Sangha events and retreats you will notice that there are jobs people take on – for example, timekeeping, taking responsibility for the shrine, washing up or co-ordinating interviews with the teacher.

Doing these jobs wholeheartedly helps strengthen our connections with each other and deepens our understanding of the Sangha, its traditions and teachings.

## Local Groups and Regional Events

There may be a local Awakened Heart Sangha group near you. If there isn't you might well wish to start one. For this you will need guidance from a member of the Shrimalagana who could help you form an introductory meditation group. You may be able to find others interested in working on *Discovering the Heart of Buddhism* with you.

*You can read more about the Shrimalagana on page 49.*

In some areas there are well-established groups explicitly working on other areas *of Living the Awakened Heart*. Groups can invite Awakened Heart Sangha teachers to lead teaching days or weekends, and can organize events where Lama Shenpen teaches. All events are related to one or more areas of *Living the Awakened Heart*.

*You can read more about Awakened Heart Sangha teachers on page 56.*

Joining a group is a way to meet fellow-students face to face, to share experiences and explore the teachings. It is an opportunity to practise with others and deepen connections to the Sangha and the teaching.

## Online Groups

Members are encouraged to connect online. This is important for those who don't live near others in the Sangha. Forums are created in order that Members can discuss their practice with others, perhaps arranging to meditate 'virtually' together, or just to connect.

*Ask Student Support for more information.*

# Deepening Your Commitment to the Sangha

In practice, if left to your own devices, you can feel a bit at sea in terms of knowing what to do next and how to focus, prioritize or galvanize your practice. You need guidance about what are the most important events or materials for you to explore at any particular stage in your learning.

So far you have been given a sense of the structure and ethos of the Awakened Heart Sangha. To deepen your connection with the Sangha, you will need a Senior Mentor, either formally or informally, who can help you to check out your understanding, answer your questions and guide you in the right direction.

For this you will need to know how to find and relate to a Mentor, what to expect and what is expected of you.

When you become a Member, you will be allocated a Mentor to help you work through *Discovering the Heart of Buddhism.* Further training courses may involve working with different Mentors, specific to the course, if one is available.

Guidance on your particular practice and Personal Pathway can be given by your Senior Mentor or Student Support, but you are encouraged to talk to Lama Shenpen at least once a year, if not more often.

## The Ganas

To help to ensure the authenticity and effectiveness of this transmission lineage, Lama Shenpen has created two circles (called "ganas" – see below) within the structure of the mandala.

Gana means an assembly and here it refers to an assembly of practitioners who practice together within the same mandala. Lama Shenpen chose this name because of a reference in the Shrimaladevi Sutra* to ganas of practitioners in the "Dark Age". The implication is that if the Members of these ganas keep good samaya connections and have faith in the Buddha then the Buddha will always be present with them and they can meet the Buddha face to face.

The two central ganas are the:

*The Mahayanagana*

*The Shrimalagana*

Belonging to a gana is training in the meaning and importance of samaya. It is the samaya between the Members of the Sangha that will hold it together over

* The Shrimaladevi Sutra is a Mahayana sutra and one of the main sources for the Tathagatagarbha doctrine concerning Buddha Nature. This is one of the main sources for the Ratnagotravibagha – the subject of Lama Shenpen's doctoral thesis and foundation for her teaching.

time and ensure the authenticity of its transmission lineage.

Gana Members need to consider the meaning of samaya carefully before asking to step into the gana circle. It is very important for the integrity of the gana that Members keep whatever commitment they make or at the very least show due regard for the others in the gana if they find themselves wanting to step out of the circle.

In the context of the Awakened Heart Sangha, the Mahayanagana including the Shrimalagana is a circle of students who keep in touch with partners on a monthly basis at the full moon. Every member of the gana commits themselves to performing a feast offering (which can be quite simple in form) and to contact their partners for Dharma companionship and support in their practice. If you wish to complete the level of learning required to be eligible for entry to the Mahayanagana or Shrimalagana, there is a specific training programme.

To be a member of a gana is a responsibility to your partners and to the gana as a whole as well as to the wider Sangha.

## The Mahayanagana

The Mahayanagana is actually made up of 2 concentric circles:

- The Main Body of the Mahayanagana. This is a circle made up of Members who have committed to working with a partner and practicing the feast offering each month. These Members commit to deepening their understanding of the *Living the Awakened Heart* training and the values, vision and ethos of the Sangha.

- The Shrimalagana – The Heart of the Mahayanagana. Those who have proven their commitment over time and have been invited to become Members who act as guardians of the mandala.

Students who feel that they are ready to deepen their connection with the Sangha can work with a Mentor on the *Feast Offering* and *Pranidhana* online modules and the *Awakening Dialogue course.*

Once they have completed this training, they can request to be invited to join the main body of the Mahayanagana. They commit to a monthly feast offering practice and discussing their practice with a partner.

Some in the Mahayanagana commit to working closely with the Shrimalagana. They also train to understand the values, vision and ethos, perhaps with an aspiration to being invited into the Shrimalagana themselves at some point.

## The Shrimalagana

Lama Shenpen has accepted vows of commitment from the Members of the Shrimalagana who have:

- Completed sufficient learning and proved their commitment over a number of years.
- Kept good samaya with her and with each other.
- Shown that they understand the vision, values and ethos of the Awakened Heart Sangha.

Lama Shenpen expects her students to look to the Members of the Shrimalagana as guardians who stand for the integrity, values and vision of the transmission lineage.

## Other Options for Members

If you are a new Member of the Awakened Heart Sangha you will normally work with a Mentor on *Discovering the Heart of Buddhism* for at least a year.

Most Members work on *Discovering the Heart of Buddhism* for at least three years and everyone will continue to spiral around the principles of *Discovering the Heart of Buddhism* indefinitely. Some join in with *Living the Awakened Heart* courses and events online or at local events and retreats, perhaps visiting the Hermitage on an annual basis and volunteering to help in various ways to support and help the Sangha's activity. This is a good option and might be the way you want to engage as a Member of the Awakened Heart Sangha for the foreseeable future.

Lama Shenpen encourages Members to form groups with other Members or link up in whatever way they can. Some students arrange ganas of their own, perhaps to do a special practice together at the full moon like the other ganas do, or continue to deepen their connection following a retreat or having taken vows together. Some choose to work through particular materials together.

*Ask Student Support for more information on joining or setting up a gana.*

# Gateways and Commitments

Each gateway has a commitment to training and a transmission.

While each transmission can be given at any stage of a student's training, it is the combination of commitment and transmission that signifies the stepping through the gateway.

Although transmission is given with the recognition that each student will only be able to understand it at the level they are at, some training or a conversation with your Mentor needs to be had before receiving a transmission.

### Gateway into 'Membership of the Mandala of the Awakened Heart Sangha':

*Entry requirement:*

- Completion of an Introduction to Formless Meditation course, including the transmission.
- Familiarity with the Discovering the Heart of Buddhism materials and the Sangha structure.

*Commitment:*

- A commitment to studying *Discovering the Heart of Buddhism* with a Mentor.
- Support the Sangha with a regular financial contribution

*Transmission:*

- Discovering the Heart of Buddhism

### Gateway into *'Membership of the Mahayanagana' Involves:*

*Entry requirements:*

*Having fulfilled the requirements to become a Member, have:*

- Been a Member for at least two years.
- Completed the Feast Offering online module.
- Completed the Pranidhana online module.
- Completed the foundation course in Awakening Dialogue.
- Had a discussion with a Senior Mentor expressing wish to step forward.

*Commitment:*

- Full moon calls with a Mayahanagana partner
- Monthly Feast Offering practice

*Transmission:*

- Feast Offering

*Those who aspire to step forward and become members of the Shrimalagana will be required to commit to a further level of training:*

Having fulfilled the requirements to become a Member of the Mahyanagana, they will also have:

- Worked with a Peer Mentor and Senior Mentor for at least 1 year.

- Sufficient experience and understanding of the *Living the Awakened Heart* training including Trusting the Heart of Buddhism.

## Commitment to training:

- Further training in values, vision and ethos

- Training as a Senior Mentor

- Working closely with the Shrimalagana

- Involved with coordinating the Main Body of the Mahayanagana and helping to organise the Annual Mahayanagana retreat/gathering

- Taking on a volunteer role or project

### *Gateway into 'Membership of the Shrimalagana':*

Membership is by invitation from Lama Shenpen in consultation with the Members of the Shrimalagana.

To stand as guardians of the mandala means to maintain its stability, ethos and vision and to be in harmony with the specific ethos and functioning of the Shrimalagana.
Lama Shenpen will personally invite Members of the Mahayanagana who she and the rest of the Shrimalagana perceive as suitable and required at any given time.

## *Entry Requirements:*

*Having fulfilled the necessary requirements as listed above they will have:*

- Been a Member of the Awakened Heart Sangha for a minimum of 5 years.
- Been recommended by a Member of the Shrimalagana as their Senior Mentor.
- Been voted in by all Members of the Shrimalagana

## *Commitment to Training:*

- Training in working with the Shrimala Trust and understanding the role of its trustees.
- Write and/or prepare a presentation on a Dharma project.

*Lifetime Commitment:*

•     Support and protect the values, vision and ethos of the Awakened Heart Sangha

•     Embody the values and ethos and to be seen as a role model for the rest of the Sangha.

*Transmission:*

• Heart Essence

# Who Are the Teachers of the Awakened Heart Sangha?

Lama Shenpen as the founding teacher of the Awakened Heart Sangha is responsible for authorizing all its teachers.

The Awakened Heart Sangha is a transmission mandala. Authorization is about protecting the authenticity of the transmission so that the power of its truth and the aliveness of its Reality can be passed on to others.

It is also about protecting the integrity of the Awakened Heart Sangha mandala as a vehicle for the teaching of the lineage so that it can be made available for future generations.

# Five Certainties

The manifestation of a Dharma teaching in the world requires the mandala of the five certainties.

- A certain teacher
- A certain time
- A certain place
- A certain teaching
- A certain assembly of students *

In the mandala of the five certainties the role of the teacher is created and affirmed by the relationship between the teacher and all those present.

In the Awakened Heart Sangha, the 'certain teachers' are those who are authorized to teach the 'certain teaching' that accords with the teachings of *Living the Awakened Heart.*

For any Sangha, consistency in approach is important. Different teachers present the Dharma in different ways according to their different styles, capacities and traditions. As a Member you have chosen the Awakened Heart Sangha approach.

---

* More can be read on this in 'Spiritual Authority in Buddhism' by Lama Shenpen, ask Student Support for more information

In the Awakened Heart Sangha we want to uphold all the essential elements of training in a genuine transmission lineage within the Kagyu-Nyingma tradition. At the same time, we need to be sensitive to the natural use of English and our cultural inheritance as Westerners living as householders in the modern world.

Authorizing teachers, therefore, is about making sure that those who teach within the Awakened Heart Sangha have sufficient understanding to ensure that their approach and language are consistent with the Awakened Heart Sangha's style and ethos. This in turn ensures that when transmission is given, it is in terms that can be recognised by other Members of the Awakened Heart Sangha and with the lineage in general.

If other teachers were to come in with an incompatible style, then even though the teacher might be good, it could lead to confusion.

Another reason for authorization is to protect the integrity of the mandala from this kind of confusion.

## Levels of Authorization

Even at the early stages of a person's entering the Awakened Heart Sangha mandala they encounter its Members. This gives them a living connection with the lineage. At any level anyone taking a mentoring or teaching role is reinforcing that living connection and some kind of transmission is already happening.

All Sangha Members need to be aware of the importance of their role in this process, and take responsibility and care for what is transmitted.

As our understanding deepens we need to look for teachers with the understanding, experience and/or realisation that corresponds to our own level.

Not all Mentors and teachers in the Awakened Heart Sangha are at the same level. Members need to use their judgment when deciding to what extent an authorized teacher's understanding is greater than their own. All Mentors and teachers in the Awakened Heart Sangha are told never to assume they know more than those they are teaching. This is their discipline.

## Teaching as Practice

Lama Shenpen encourages her students to take on various teaching roles as a way to deepen their practice. She calls this *'teaching as practice'*. Teaching others can really help us to integrate and absorb what we have learnt.

This doesn't necessarily need formal authorization. It might simply involve being asked to present a story or teaching at a Sangha gathering as a one-off event.

For example, even new students are invited to take the teacher's chair to tell life stories at retreats. The person telling the story is taking the role of the teacher and takes that place in the mandala.

Another example would be working as a Peer Mentor with another Member on an online course.

## Mentoring

Having trained for some time within the Awakened Heart Sangha, Members have the opportunity to train to become a Mentor in a more specific sense. This is first level of authorization within the Awakened Heart Sangha. As well as being a service for the Sangha becoming a Mentor is a good way of deepening your own practice and understanding. All Members work with a Mentor as they study *Discovering the Heart of Buddhism* and require support in all areas of their training. Trained Mentors are therefore essential for the mandala to continue as a vehicle for the teaching and transmission. If you would like to learn more about becoming a Mentor please contact Student Support.

Members wishing to set up a local group are encouraged to become authorized Local Group Mentors and receive further training and guidance from the Shrimalagana.

## The Teaching Role of the Shrimalagana

When students enter the Shrimalagana they have been trained to a recognized level and have shown the commitment, understanding and other qualities needed to be able to stand for the values of the Awakened Heart Sangha. They have received the necessary transmissions and so are authorized to teach within the Awakened Heart Sangha mandala to the level of their individual competence.

## Visiting Teachers

From time to time Lama Shenpen invites teachers from other Sanghas to teach in the Awakened Heart Sangha. These teachers are an important source of knowledge, experience, advice and inspiration.

Importantly Lama Shenpen invites her own teachers, Khenpo Tsultrim Gyamtso Rinpoche and Rigdzin Shikpo Rinpoche to teach from time to time.

## Teaching at Local Groups

Local groups are encouraged to invite Awakened Heart Sangha teachers. Student Support can give advice on how to invite teachers. Anyone who wishes to set up a local group should ask Student Support for current guidelines and advice.

# After Lama Shenpen

The Shrimalagana already has responsibility for the values, vision and ethos, training and authorization of Mentors and teachers for the Awakened Heart Sangha. They hold this role, recognizing that as long as Lama Shenpen is alive they will exercise this responsibility by deferring to her and following her advice and leadership.

Once she is gone they will continue in the same role. They will decide who is suitable to teach in the Awakened Heart Sangha so that its values are protected and maintained.

Individual Members will need to respect the decisions of the Shrimalagana in relation to the activity of the Sangha, but may still approach other teachers for guidance.

It is possible for Members to combine being the student of another Lama with being a Member of the Awakened Heart Sangha.

# Personal Contribution

## Financial Support

For the Awakened Heart Sangha to be sustainable, make the Hermitage available as a Sacred Space and support the activity of Lama Shenpen, including the training of a new generation of teachers, it requires a financial commitment from its Members and its Supporting Friends.

The question of how much you are able and willing to give is another matter to discuss with Student Support.

You will need to think about this in a very honest and deep manner.

In traditional Buddhist cultures one makes offerings to teachers and practitioners as an integral part of one's own spiritual practice.

This is also true for us in the Awakened Heart Sangha. Our Membership donation is an expression of our generosity and commitment to each other and our teachers; it has symbolic as well as financial value.

What is different for us is the way we go about it. We can do what is more normal in our culture, which is to make regular donations to a charity (in this case *The Shrimala Trust*, which supports Lama Shenpen's Dharma activity and the Awakened Heart Sangha).

It is the generosity of its Members and Supporting Friends that allows the whole mandala to function effectively. It is able to do this as long as we, the Members, are committed to giving our time and money as generously as we can.

*You can read more about The Shrimala Trust on page 70.*

## Becoming a Supporting Friend

You are welcome to become a Supporting Friend by making an annual or monthly donation of your choice or volunteering and participating at events and local groups.

Whether you become a Supporting Friend or not you are welcome to join a local group and come along to certain retreats and events. You can continue to receive Buddhism Connect and listen to selected recordings and videos, read newsletter updates including news from Lama Shenpen. There won't be the same level of expectation of you as for a Member.

# Membership of the Awakened Heart Sangha

The Members of the Awakened Heart Sangha form a community. Members support the vision and activity of Lama Shenpen in order to benefit each other's deepening practice.

As Members, we depend on each other for the mandala to be sustainable and to thrive. In order for any activity to take place, either online, regionally or at the Hermitage, Members and friends are needed to organize them and help out. Commitment, financial support and volunteering are what keep the Dharma activity of the Awakened Heart Sangha flowing for the benefit of its Members and others.

For each of us personally it is vital for our practice that we establish a strong connection with a teaching mandala. This links us into the vast power of the lineage that pulls us to Awakening. We establish this connection by making a commitment to engage in a clear, open and sensitive relationship (an energy exchange) with the teaching mandala. From our side we give our practice, service and resources. This energises the mandala so that Dharma flows back from it to us.

As we come to recognise that we are involved in a teaching mandala, we also realise its importance for others as well as ourselves. We feel a corresponding sense of responsibility for helping it continue and for making it as effective as possible.

Our own practice, practising with others, helping and supporting teachers and helping to create teaching, learning and practice situations are all means of creating a powerful and effective teaching mandala.

This is not simply for ourselves or even this time and place, but for all future generations and worlds without end.

Membership is for those who want to engage with the Awakened Heart Sangha in a strong and stable way for the foreseeable future. It is not necessarily a lifetime commitment, although it could be if you wish. It is more a recognition that the Awakened Heart Sangha is currently your 'spiritual home' or 'Dharma family'. We become the community you are primarily and seriously practising with.

Within the community, our life circumstances vary and we cannot always practise or give as much as we would like but we can still feel a sense of deep involvement with the Sangha. Becoming a Member is how we communicate this. Membership therefore indicates a connection that is not dependent on the details of our life situation, such as how many courses we can get to in a particular year, but is a source of spiritual support through the ups and downs of our lives.

# Regular Membership Donations

It can be difficult to decide how much to give. As a Member it is important to think about this. A fixed sum is not stipulated, since we find ourselves in diverse financial circumstances. For example, some Members are able to donate more than others due to their life circumstances but are unable to give time to run events. Some are unable to donate as much as they would like, but are very able to give time and energy to their practice and to run events or compile teaching materials.

It is more about the spirit in which we give than exactly how much we give.

The table on the following page might help to give you an idea of what financial contribution you might offer at this time in your life.

These figures are a general guide and not exact calculations

| | |
|---|---|
| £10-£30 per month | If the majority of Members were to donate this amount, the activity of the Sangha would be heavily reliant on those who could afford to be more generous. |
| £30-£60 per month | If the majority of Members were to donate this amount, the activity of the Sangha could be sustained at its present level. |
| More than £60 per month | If the majority of Members were to donate this amount, the activity of the Sangha could be developed and sustained into the future. |

# Where Do Membership Contributions Go?

The Awakened Heart Sangha is supported in its activity by *The Shrimala Trust*, a registered charity set up for this specific purpose. Its stated aim is to promote Dharma study, contemplation and meditation. The trustees of The Shrimala Trust are responsible for its finances and make sure that they are spent in accordance with the aims of the charity. This means that it supports the Awakened Heart Sangha under the direction of the Dharma Director, Lama Shenpen Hookham. The annual accounts are available to Members of the Awakened Heart Sangha on request; they are posted onto the Members' forums and the Charity Commission website.

An Annual General Meeting is held each year and all Members are invited to attend.

Members are kept informed about and are encouraged to become involved with and contribute to future plans by engaging with the vision and five-year plan that is updated each year and posted on the Members' forum.

## What If I Am Not Ready for Membership Right Now?

As mentioned earlier, you may take up to a year before formally becoming a Member, requesting transmission and entering the gateway proper, while still being able to work with a Mentor and being engaged with *Discovering the Heart of Buddhism*.

At the end of this year, you may want to maintain your connection with the Awakened Heart Sangha but not feel ready to commit yourself to Membership and all it implies at this point.

There are still many ways in which you can maintain your connection to the Sangha and benefit from Lama Shenpen's teachings, for example, by becoming a Supporting Friend.

## Honorary Membership

Sometimes we invite practitioners committed to other Sanghas to become Honorary Members of the Awakened Heart Sangha in recognition of their commitment to Dharma. This enriches both their mandalas and ours.

## What Do I Do Next?

If you feel that you are ready to make the step into becoming a Member of the Awakened Heart Sangha, you can contact Student Support who will let you know where to go from here.

If you would like to become a Supporting Friend you can make a regular donation via the website.

# Contact Information

*Hermitage and Lama Shenpen's office*

*Hermitage of the Awakened Heart*
*Ynys Graianog*
*Ynys*
*Criccieth*
*LL52 0NT*
*T: 01766 530 839*
*e: hermitage@ahs.org.uk*
*www.ahs.org.uk*

*Student Support*
*e: studentsupport@ahs.org.uk*

*To make an appointment with Lama Shenpen*
*e: tara@ahs.org.uk*

*The Shrimala Trust:*
*Registered office as above.*
*Charity Number: 1078783*
*Limited Company Number: 3880647*

# Book List

*Other Books available from Lama Shenpen and the Awakened Heart Sangha*

### Living the Awakened Heart Materials:

*Introduction to Formless Meditation*
*Formless Meditation – guided meditation CD*

### Discovering the Heart of Buddhism:
*Core Themes*
*Indestructible Heart Essence*
*Confidence*
*Heart Wish*
*Openness*
*Clarity*
*Sensitivity*
*Mandala Principle*

### Trusting the Heart of Buddhism:
*Book One*
*Book Two*

*Living the Awakened Heart*
*The Feast Offering*
*Samantabadracharya Pranidhana*
*The Shrimala Devi Sutra*
*Four Songs of Milarepa*
*Apramanas Booklet*
*Mandala of Sacred Space*
*The Awakened Heart Sangha liturgy - In Praise of the Three Jewels CD*
*Taking Refuge Booklet*
*Bodhisattva Vow Booklet*
*There's more to Dying than Death*
*An Introduction to Awakened Heart Sangha Events Booklet*

*The Hermitage of the Awakened Heart Booklet*
*Spiritual Authority in Buddhism*

**Books by Rigdzin Shikpo:**

*Openness Clarity Sensitivity*
*Mahayana Sutra Principles*

*For more details including prices and availability, please contact Student Support.*

*The cover picture is an abstract from a picture called "A detail of 'Primordial Purity, Golden World' by Contemporary Tibetan Calligraphy Artist Tashi Mannox: (photo by Malcolm Payne of Colourfast Imaging) www.tashimannox.com.*

*Tashi apprenticed under the direction of a master of Tibetan art, the late Sherab Palden Beru. Part of Tashi's training was in the elaborate art of temple decoration, which is the traditionally hub for the Tibetan arts and its deep symbolism.*

*Since laying down his monastic robes in 2000, Tashi has built on his disciplined training and arising spiritual awareness, formed through years of practising meditation and Buddhist philosophy - to produce a collection of iconographic masterpieces that reveal powerful, sacred themes through the majestic images of Tibetan Buddhist iconography.*

*Tashi has known Lama Shenpen since childhood.*

*Publication date - ©2015*

Notes:

Notes:

Notes:

Notes:

Notes:

Notes:

Notes:

Notes:

Notes:

Notes:

Notes:

Notes:

Notes:

Notes:

Notes:

Notes:

Notes:

Notes:

Notes:

Notes:

Notes:

Notes:

Notes:

Notes:

Made in the USA
Charleston, SC
13 May 2015